E. LAZZARO

101 Facts about Sharks

Contents

1

Introduction

W elcome to 101 Facts about Sharks! This book is a tribute to my son Oliver, whose passion for sharks ignited during a school project and has since spread throughout our household. His enthusiasm has inspired us to delve deeper into the fascinating world of sharks, prompting the creation of this book to share our newfound love with others.

In these pages, we will plunge into the depths of the great blue ocean to uncover captivating insights about one of Earth's oldest and most enigmatic creatures: sharks. Sharks have patrolled our planet's waters for over 400 million years, predating even the dinosaurs. Sharks have evolved into some of Earth's most efficient and awe-inspiring predators through evolutionary marvels, such as their powerful bodies, extraordinary adaptations, and acute senses.

Whether you're an ardent shark aficionado like Oliver or a curious student eager to learn more, this book is crafted for you. We aim to provide an engaging exploration of sharks, covering everything from their diverse habitats and unique feeding behaviors to the intricacies of their life cycles. Along the way, we'll nod to their presence in pop culture, showcasing their enduring fascination in our society.

So, let's embark on this adventure together and delve into 101 Facts about Sharks! Get ready to be captivated by the wonders of these remarkable creatures that continue to intrigue and inspire us all.

2

Quick Facts Everyone Should Know!

I f you only have time to explore one chapter, you've landed on the perfect place! Here, we've curated a collection of fascinating facts to pique your interest and arm you with intriguing tidbits to impress your friends and family.

Sharks, the ancient rulers of the oceans, have captivated human imagination for centuries. Their unparalleled adaptability and finely honed senses make them some of the most efficient predators in the animal kingdom.

Sharks exhibit incredible adaptations tailored to their environments and diverse habitats. Some species, like the great white shark, can breach the water surface with astonishing agility, while others, like the whale shark, peacefully filter-feed on plankton with their massive mouths.

Beyond their biological marvels, sharks have left an indelible mark on human culture and imagination. They feature prominently in ancient myths and legends, symbolizing fear and respect. Sharks continue to capture our fascination in modern times, appearing in literature, art, and even blockbuster movies.

So, dive into this chapter and uncover these quick facts that highlight the extraordinary world of sharks. Whether you're sharing these insights with friends or expanding your knowledge, you will surely be amazed by the depth of wonder sharks bring to our planet's waters.

Fact #1—Sharks have roamed the Earth for over 400 million years, predating even the dinosaurs. They have survived multiple mass extinctions throughout their long history, demonstrating remarkable resilience and adaptability.

Fact # 2- Sharks, encompassing over 500 known species, represent one of the ocean's most diverse and ancient groups of fish. This vast array of species spans a wide range of sizes, from the diminutive dwarf lantern shark, which measures only about 8 inches, to the colossal whale shark, reaching up to 40 feet in height.

Fact #3- Sharks have no bones! Their skeletons are made of cartilage, which makes them lighter and more flexible.

Fact #4- Sharks possess a fascinating adaptation known as the ampullae of Lorenzini, specialized organs that allow them to detect weak electric fields generated by living organisms in their environment. One of the most remarkable uses is locating prey that may be hidden or camouflaged, such as fish buried in the sand or under rocks. Sharks can effectively pinpoint their location by sensing the electric fields produced by the muscle contractions of these potential meals without relying solely on visual cues. This sensory advantage is particularly advantageous in murky or dark waters with limited visibility.

Fact #5- Sharks possess an exceptional sense of smell, crucial in their daily lives and for survival strategies. Their olfactory abilities are finely tuned, allowing them to detect tiny amounts of scent molecules dissolved in the water, sometimes in concentrations as low as one part per million. This heightened sense of smell serves multiple critical functions in their underwater world. Sharks use their sense of smell to navigate and recognize territorial markers within their habitat. By detecting chemical signals left behind by conspecifics, they can identify established territories, potential threats, or areas abundant with food resources.

Fact #6- Humans aren't on a shark's menu! Shark attacks or bites are a case of mistaken identity. Sharks mistake humans for seals or dolphins.

Fact #7- Humans are one of the biggest threats to sharks, responsible for over 100 million sharks killed a year through overfishing, bycatching and habitat destruction.

Fact #8- Sharks are essential to maintain the health of marine ecosystems. As apex predators, they support healthy fish populations and prevent fallout from fish overpopulating.

3

Shark Habitats

While sharks commonly inhabit the vast expanses of the ocean, their adaptability extends far beyond marine environments. Contrary to popular belief, sharks can also venture into freshwater habitats, such as lakes and certain rivers, showcasing their remarkable ability to adapt to varied ecological niches.

Moreover, sharks exhibit surprising versatility in terms of temperature preferences. While some species inhabit icy polar regions, others thrive in the warm, sun-drenched waters of the tropics. This wide-ranging habitat diversity underscores their evolutionary success and resilience in adapting to different climates and conditions.

From the freezing depths of polar seas to the balmy shallows of tropical reefs, sharks exemplify nature's adaptability and resilience. Their presence in such diverse habitats enriches our understanding of their ecological roles and underscores the importance of conservation efforts to protect these awe-inspiring creatures across their entire range.

Fact #9—Sharks can only be found in about 30% of the oceans, making most of the Earth shark-free.

Fact #10- Sharks that live in the open ocean, or the "pelagic zone," have adapted to become fast swimmers to keep up with prey. One example is the shortfin mako shark, which can swim up to 50 miles per hour.

Fact #11- Goblin sharks prefer the dark and live in the deep ocean, up to 1300 m down! Their long snout is covered with particular organs that help them locate prey by sensing the electric field created by fish in dim lighting.

Fact #12- Reef sharks prefer the warm waters of the Caribbean, often shaping the local ecosystem. They help maintain healthy fish communities and prevent overpopulation. Healthy reefs are more resilient to overcoming stressors like coral disease and climate change.

Fact #13- Angel and Hammerhead sharks have long, flat heads and bodies to help sense prey within the sandy bottom of their habitat. They are often found in shallow waters near continental shelves like the Mediterranean Sea or eastern Atlantic.

Fact #14- Lemon sharks prefer fresh and ocean waters, commonly found in Florida'sulf and Atlantic coasts. This shark migrates south for the winter months.

Fact #15—While most think sharks can't be found in freshwater, bull sharks prefer freshwater. They are commonly found in Australian and Southeast Asian rivers and only venture into saltwater when reproducing.

4

Shark Families

Sharks are fascinating creatures belonging to the Chondrichthyes classification, which distinguishes them as cartilaginous fish, unlike bony fish. This means that their skeletons are made of cartilage rather than bone, a feature that offers them greater flexibility and lighter weight, aiding in their survival in diverse marine environments. The Chondrichthyes classification is further divided into two sub-groups: Holocephali and Elasmobranchii. Each of these sub-groups encompasses species with unique characteristics, allowing for a more precise understanding of the vast diversity within the shark family.

Fact #16: Holocephali sharks have four-gill slits with a cover called an operculum. Their jaws are also fused to their skulls. Common names include ghost sharks, ratfish, rabbitfish, and spookfish.

Fact #17- Elasmobranchii sharks have five to seven-gill slits and an upper jaw that is detached from their skulls. They have multiple rows of teeth which continue to be replaced. There are eight sub-categories of Elasmobranchii- Carcharhiniformes, Heterodontiformes, Hexanchiformes, Lamniformes, Orectolobiformes, Pristiophoriformes, Squaliformes, and Squatiniformes.

Fact #18- Caracharhiniformes sharks are the largest group of sharks. They have 5-gill slits, two dorsal fins, an anal fin, a wide mouth with shark teeth, and moveable eyelids. Common examples include bull shark, giant hammerhead shark, and tiger shark.

Fact #19- Heterodontiformes sharks are a small group of sharks, with only nine species known. They have five-gill slits, a strong spine with a dorsal fin, and both flat rounded and sharp teeth. Common examples include horn sharks.

Fact #20- Hexanchiformes sharks are the most primitive sharks alive today. They can have either six or seven-gill slits, thorny teeth, a single dorsal fin, and an anal fin. They tend to live in the deep, cold water. One example is a sharpnose sevengill shark.

Fact #21- Lamniformes sharks have five-gill slits and a wide mouth with several rows of sharp teeth. They also have two dorsal fins and an anal fin. They can maintain a higher body temperature than the water around them. Common Lamniformes sharks include longfin mako sharks, crocodile sharks, and white sharks.

Fact #22- Orectolobiformes sharks include some of the most diverse sharks. They have five-gill slits, an anal fin, and two spineless dorsal fins, and some have barbels on their chins. Most have patterned skin, and all have spiracles near their eyes. Common Orectolobiformes sharks include zebra sharks, nurse sharks, and spotted wobbegong.

Fact #23- Pristiophoriformes sharks are also known as saw sharks for their saw-like snouts. They have four or six-gill slits, expansive pectoral fins, two dorsal fins, and traverse teeth. These sharks prefer tropical coastal waters. One example is the Bahamas sawshark.

Fact #24- Squaliformes sharks can be found in nearly all marine habitats. These sharks have five-gill slits, two dorsal fins, and a long snout with a short mouth. Those that live in the deep water can even be bioluminescent. Some examples include the great lantern shark, Greenland shark, and spiny dogfish.

Fact #25- Squatiniformes sharks have eyes and spiracles on their head, nasal barbels, flattened bodies, and a mouth with dermal flaps covering the short snout. Angel sharks are a common Squatiniformes.

5

Shark Teeth

Sharks are renowned as the deadliest predators in the ocean, instilling both awe and fear due to their formidable hunting capabilities. Their impressive teeth are central to their predatory prowess, which is crucial in their ability to capture and kill prey efficiently. But what exactly composes these teeth, and what features make them so deadly?

Fact #26- Shark teeth are composed primarily of a hard mineralized substance known as calcium phosphate, specifically in the form of hydroxyapatite. This mineral composition gives shark teeth characteristic durability and sharpness, essential for their role as predatory tools in the marine environment.

Fact #27- Sharks can not get cavities and, instead, shed their teeth. On average, sharks lose about one tooth per week of their life. This tooth can be replaced in as little as 24 hours.

Fact #28- Many sharks have multiple rows of teeth, with the lower being pointed and the upper rows being more triangular. Some sharks have as many as 50 rows of teeth!

Fact #29- Whales and basking sharks have over 3,000 tiny teeth that act as filters to gather up plankton to eat, similar to whales.

Fact #30- Nurse sharks have dense, flat teeth, perfect for crushing crabs or other shelled sea creatures.

Fact #31- The arrangement of bull shark teeth reflects their predatory strategy. Their upper and lower jaws contain rows of closely spaced, sharp teeth interning when the jaws close. This dental configuration is ideal for grasping slippery fish and squid, preventing them from escaping once caught. The slender shape of their teeth also facilitates piercing through the flesh of their prey with minimal resistance, ensuring quick and adequate feeding.

Fact #32- Shark teeth are popular to collect and trade, with Megalodon teeth being the most valuable. You can find more shark teeth in Venice, Florida, than anywhere else.

Fact #33- Shark teeth used to be used as tools for cutting food, carving, and digging.

6

Hunting and Feeding

With their well-earned reputation as deadly killers, sharks are undeniably the ocean's most formidable hunters. These apex predators are highly adapted to their environments, exhibiting a wide range of hunting habits that vary significantly by shark type, reflecting their preferred habitats and the prey they target.

Their diverse hunting habits, tailored to their specific environments and prey, advanced sensory capabilities, and powerful, agile bodies make them unparalleled predators in the marine world. Sharks continue to reign supreme as the apex predators of the sea, whether through swift ambushes, stealthy tracking, or sheer endurance.

Fact #34- Often referred to as the "garbage can of the sea," tiger sharks are opportunistic feeders. They have been known to feed on everything from bony fish to other sharks and even sea turtles.

Fact #35- Sharks, as apex predators of the ocean, exhibit a feeding behavior finely tuned to their energy requirements and prey availability in their environment. On average, sharks consume between 1% and 10% of their body weight per week, depending on species, size, metabolic rate, and the abundance of food sources.

Fact #36- Most sharks swallow their food whole, no chewing!

Fact #37- Whale sharks filter feed and can filter 4,000 gallons of water per hour.

Fact #38- Nurse sharks, known for their distinctive appearance and gentle demeanor, employ a unique feeding strategy that showcases their remarkable adaptations for hunting in reef environments. Central to their hunting technique is suction generated by their thick, fleshy lips to extract prey from holes and crevices within coral reefs and rocky substrates.

These sharks possess potent jaws and muscular lips that create a vacuum-like effect when pressed against surfaces. This suction capability allows nurse sharks to effectively dislodge and consume a variety of prey that seek shelter in tight spaces, such as crustaceans, mollusks, and small fish. By leveraging their specialized anatomy, nurse sharks can access prey that might otherwise be inaccessible to predators lacking such adaptations.

Fact #39- Cookiecutter sharks first suction themselves to large fish or whales. Once complete, they use their large triangular teeth to carve out flesh.

Fact #40- Pygmy sharks, despite their diminutive size, undertake a remarkable nightly journey from the ocean's surface to the depths of the sea floor, covering nearly 5,000 feet in search of food. This vertical migration is a crucial aspect of their feeding behavior and reflects their adaptation to the dynamics of the marine environment.

Fact #41- The thresher shark hunts in pairs or groups. They circle the school of fish, herding them until they hit them with a powerful blow, up to 50 miles per hour, stunning the fish.

Fact #42- The most common hunting technique is pinning. This is when the shark pins the prey before devouring.

7

Life Cycles of a Shark

Sharks have a varied and fascinating life cycle that reflects their remarkable resilience and adaptability to their marine environments. Understanding these life cycles is crucial for ensuring the health and balance of aquatic ecosystems, as sharks play a vital role in maintaining ecological stability.

Fact # 43-Female sharks let male sharks know they are ready to mate by releasing pheromones. Male sharks then show interest in a female shark by biting her.

Fact #44- Baby sharks are called pups.

Fact #45- Most sharks give birth to live pups and are either ovo-viviparous or viviparous.

Fact #46- Ovoviviparous sharks are the most common. The embryos hatch inside the female shark and receive nutrients from its mother through a large yolk sac attached to its body. Common examples include great white, tiger, and shortfin mako sharks.

Fact #47- Viviparous shark embryos receive nutrients from their mother through an umbilical cord in their mother's uterus, similar to placental mammals. Some examples include bull sharks and hammerhead sharks.

Fact # 48- Oviparity sharks lay eggs in egg cases known as "mermaid's purses." This is only found in about 25% of sharks. Common examples include horn sharks and catsharks.

Fact #49- Shark pregnancies can last anywhere from 9 months to a year.

Fact #50- Eggs laid by sharks can take up to a year to hatch.

8

Fastest Sharks

I n the vast and mysterious oceans that cover the Earth, few creatures can match sharks' swimming prowess and maneuverability. These remarkable predators are engineered for speed and agility, with adaptations that allow them to glide effortlessly through the water. Their sleek, hydrodynamic bodies, lower body density, and powerful, muscular tails make swimming a natural and efficient endeavor for them. As apex predators, sharks dominate their aquatic realm with astonishing swiftness, cementing their reputation as some of the most efficient hunters in the ocean. This section will delve into the characteristics and capabilities of some of the world's fastest sharks, exploring how their unique adaptations enable them to achieve such remarkable speeds.

Fact #51- The hammerhead sharks are clocking in at an impressive 20 mph. They use their speed to locate and catch their preferred prey, crustaceans.

Fact #52- Bull sharks prefer the "bump and bite" method of catching prey. First, they bump into their prey, and if they seem edible, they will attack using their impressive speed of up to 25 mph.

Fact #53- Despite the nurse shark's speed of up to 25 mph, these sharks prefer crustaceans as prey. They can be found at the bottom of the ocean floor.

Fact #54- Thresher sharks prefer to stay in the deep ocean. That's fortunate as their bodies can reach up to 32 feet long and swim upwards of 30 mph.

Fact #55- While the great white shark has over 300 teeth, its speed of up to 35 mph makes this shark the ultimate apex predator.

Fact #56- The blue shark attacks its prey from underneath, using its muscular tail to reach up to 43 mph, catching prey off-guard.

Fact #57- Spinner sharks hunt prey by swimming with schools of fish and jumping and spinning out of water, creating confusion. These leaps can be over 44 mph.

Fact #58- Believed to be Earth's fastest shark, the shortfin mako shark can reach up to 60 mph for short bursts and consistently swims an average of 31 mph.

9

Shark Migration

Shark migration offers a captivating glimpse into these apex predators' mysterious and nomadic existence. Far beneath the ocean's surface, sharks undertake epic journeys that span thousands of miles, guided solely by instinct and environmental cues. These migrations serve several essential purposes, such as locating optimal feeding grounds, finding mating opportunities, and adapting to seasonal changes in their environment.

Fact #59- Three significant factors explain why sharks migrate: seasonal changes, reproduction, and food sources.

Fact #60- Seasonal changes cause sharks to migrate for more favorable weather and warmer water. Since most sharks are cold-blooded, they must move to water in their preferred temperature range. Some sharks have a higher metabolic rate that allows them to generate their own heat.

Fact #61—Food source is a common cause of migration, as sharks tend to follow the migration of their prey. One example is the great white shark, which can be found off the coast of San Francisco right after seal mating season.

Fact #62- Similar to other animals, sharks migrate to mate and give birth. One example includes the sandbar shark, who migrate from the coast of Florida to the Delaware Bay to have their pups. They then stay in this relatively safe area until they are ready to migrate south, usually in September as winter approaches.

Fact #63—Climate change has affected how sharks migrate. As water temperature continues to rise, sharks are pushed closer to the poles to find cooler waters, and they are pushed closer to the shorelines to find prey.

10

Shark Senses

Sharks possess an extraordinary array of seven senses that elevate them to apex predators in the ocean. These senses include sight, smell, taste, touch, hearing, electroreception, and the lateral line system, each contributing uniquely to their unparalleled hunting prowess.

Fact #64—Sharks possess remarkable visual capabilities that vary depending on water conditions. In optimal circumstances, they can see distances of up to 50 meters or more. Their ability to perceive their surroundings is influenced by factors such as water clarity, light levels, and the specific adaptations of their eyes.

Fact # 65- Sharks have a third eyelid, the nictitating membrane, which can slide over the eye for protection during feeding.

Fact #66- This distinct anatomical feature reflects the different functions and adaptations of the shark's sensory system compared to terrestrial animals.

Fact # 67- Sharks have a fantastic sense of smell. They can even smell a drop of blood in a pool, making their smell 100 million times better than a human.

Fact #68- Sharks often employ a unique hunting strategy where they bite their prey first to determine if it is edible. This behavior, sometimes called a "test bite" or "exploratory bite," allows sharks to gather sensory information about the potential meal. By using their highly sensitive taste buds and oral structures, sharks can assess the texture, fat content, and overall suitability of the prey before deciding whether to continue feeding.

Fact #69- Sharks react especially to low frequencies, usually in the 25 to 600-hertz range from great distances, essential for locating prey, avoiding predators, and communicating with other sharks. The inner ear's sensitivity to sound complements the shark's lateral line system, enhancing its ability to sense and respond to its environment.

Fact #70- Like humans, Shark hearing is crucial in maintaining balance and orientation. The shark's inner ear facilitates this remarkable sensory ability, structurally similar to that of humans and other vertebrates. The inner ear comprises a series of fluid-filled canals and sensory cells that detect changes in the shark's position and movement.

Fact #80- Sharks possess susceptible skin that allows them to detect even the slightest movements in their surroundings. This sensitivity is due to a network of specialized sensory cells embedded within their skin, known as mechanoreceptors. These cells are incredibly attuned to changes in water pressure and can pick up on disturbances as minute as 0.02 millimeters.

This heightened sense of touch enables sharks to feel the faintest vibrations in the water, such as those produced by the movements of prey, the approach of potential threats, or changes in the environment. This sensitivity is instrumental in limited visibility in murky or dark waters, allowing sharks to rely on tactile information to locate prey and navigate their surroundings.

The mechanoreceptors are concentrated along the shark's lateral line, a series of fluid-filled canals running along the sides of their bodies from head to tail. This lateral line system acts like a highly tuned radar, providing the shark with continuous information about the position, speed, and direction of objects around them. This ability to sense minute movements with such precision enhances their hunting efficiency and helps them maintain their status as apex predators in the ocean.

Fact #81- Sharks' electroreception allows them to detect the faint electrical signals emitted by other animals, giving them a distinct advantage in murky waters.

Fact #82- When a shark loses a scent while hunting, it will swim in a "S" pattern until it can find the trail again.

Fact #83-Sharks not only use their sense of smell when hunting but also when seeking a mate. Female sharks release pheromones that male sharks can smell.

Fact #84- Other animals, such as the platypus and bumblebee, also use electroreception. Sharks are more sensitive, though.

Fact #85- Sharks possess an extraordinary ability to avoid predators and locate prey by creating an electrical "map" of their surroundings, a skill made possible by their specialized sense known as electroreception. This remarkable adaptation is facilitated by the ampullae of Lorenzini, a network of tiny, jelly-filled pores around their snouts and heads. These pores can detect the faint electrical fields of all living organisms, including the muscle contractions and heartbeats of potential prey or the presence of other predators.

Sharks can construct a detailed map of their environment by interpreting these electrical signals, even without visual cues. This ability is particularly advantageous in the vast and often murky ocean, where visibility can be limited. The electrical map enables sharks to track prey movements over considerable distances, navigate complex underwater landscapes, and avoid potential threats.

This sophisticated sensory system also allows sharks to undertake long migrations across the ocean without losing their way. They can follow electrical cues and geomagnetic fields to reach feeding grounds, breeding sites, or warmer waters, demonstrating impressive spatial awareness and navigational precision. Through electroreception, sharks are equipped with an unparalleled ability to understand and interact with their environment, solidifying their role as one of the most adept and successful predators in the marine world.

Fact #86- The tapetum lucidum is a remarkable layer of reflective crystals situated behind the retina in a shark's eye. This specialized structure plays a crucial role in enhancing the shark's vision, particularly in the dimly lit depths of the ocean. By reflecting incoming light through the retina, the tapetum lucidum amplifies the available light, allowing sharks to see more clearly in low-light conditions. This adaptation is especially beneficial for nocturnal hunting and navigating the dark ocean waters, giving sharks a significant advantage in detecting prey and avoiding obstacles. The tapetum lucidum is a critical component of the shark's visual system, demonstrating the incredible evolutionary adaptations that have enabled these predators to thrive in their underwater environment.

Fact #87- Shark's eyes are ten times more light-sensitive than a human's.

11

Threats to Sharks

Sharks are an important part of the marine ecosystem, maintaining the balance needed for healthy marine life. Despite this, sharks increasingly face endangerment. Overfishing, bycatching, habitat destruction, and the increasing demand for shark fins have led to significant decreases in shark populations. This decrease not only impacts sharks but also affects the delicate balance of marine food webs. Understanding these impacts is essential to further conservation efforts, ensuring the survival of marine ecosystems.

Fact #88- Overfishing, the most common threat to sharks, is when fish are taken faster than they reproduce.

Fact #89- Overfishing has increased in recent years due to the massive demand for shark fins and meat. Three common sharks are spiny dogfish, porbeagle, and great hammerhead sharks.

Fact: #90- 121 classes of sharks are considered endangered.

Fact #91- 90 classes of sharks are considered critically endangered.

Fact #92- 180 classes are considered vulnerable.

Fact #93- Bycatching is when sharks are not the target of fishing but are caught anyway. A common occurrence is fishing for tuna, swordfish, halibut, or cod.

Fact #94- Fisheries are responsible for about 100 million shark deaths annually. In comparison, sharks only kill an average of 10 humans a year.

Fact #95- Coral reefs are affected by sedimentation and fertilizer runoff from farmland and climate change. This dramatically impacts the volume of prey available for sharks.

Fact #96- Approximately 25% of the earth's shark species residing on coastal continental shelves are threatened by extinction.

Fact #97-Ten of the most endangered shark species include the pondicherry shark, lost shark, Ganges shark, daggernose shark, sand tiger shark, oceanic whitetip, scalloped hammerhead, short-tail nurse shark, great hammerhead, and angel sharks.

Fact #98- To mitigate overfishing and bycatch, organizations like the WWF have partnered with the world's largest fishing management companies and local authorities to create and implement governing laws.

Fact #99- The Convention on the Conservation Migratory Species of Wild Animals, also known as CMS, was created for sharks and all aquatic, avian, and terrestrial migratory species. It is an intergovernmental treaty concerned with the conservation of habitats and wildlife globally and is backed by the United Nations Environment Programme.

Fact #100- Sharks were first added to the Convention on International Trade in Endangered Species of Wild Fauna and Flora (CITES) in 2003. The first sharks added were the basking shark and whale shark.

Fact #101- You can take action by donating to organizations like WWF and even adopting a shark!

12

Conclusion

Sharks are extraordinary creatures that have roamed the oceans for hundreds of millions of years, embodying both the beauty and the complexity of marine life. Through the fascinating facts and insights presented in this book, we have delved into the diverse species of sharks, their unique adaptations, and their critical roles in the ocean's ecosystems. As we gain a deeper understanding of these apex predators, it becomes increasingly clear that their preservation is essential for the health of our oceans and the overall balance of life on Earth. By promoting awareness and supporting conservation efforts, we can help ensure that future generations will continue to marvel at the awe-inspiring world of sharks. Let us all be inspired to protect and cherish these magnificent beings, safeguarding their place in the natural world.

Thank you for reading; we hope you enjoyed it! Please leave a review on Amazon to tell us how we did.

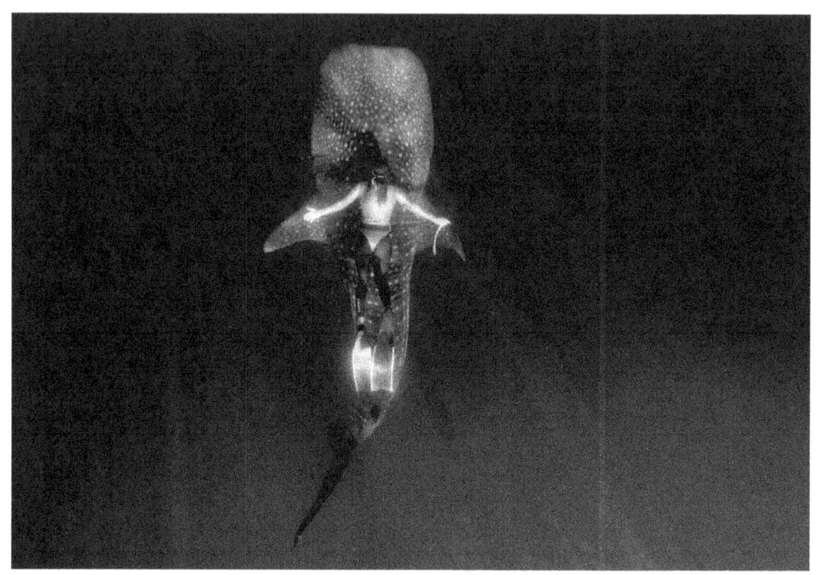

13

Resources

Marine Sanctuary Foundation. (2023, March 31). Sharks: fact or fiction? | National Marine Sanctuary Foundation. National Marine Sanctuary Foundation. https://marines anctuary.org/blog/sharks-fact-or-fiction/?gad_source=1&gclid=Cj0 KCQjwkdO0BhDxARIsANkNcrd_5eDGuzk_ujeJTnP-YEHswHVH9 ghEC1ODuXF52_EAez7OyiQA-w0aAgnIEALw_wcB

Shark Senses. (n.d.). The Shark Trust. https://www.sharktrust.org/ shark-senses

ED_BluePlanet. (2019, June 24). Where do sharks live? Fun facts about shark habitat. https://www.blueplanetaquarium.com/sharks/where-do-sharks-live/

Oceana. (2024, May 17). Goblin Shark | Oceana. https://oceana.org/ marine-life/goblin-shark/

Reef Sharks. (n.d.). WWF. https://www.wwfca.org/en/species/reef_ sharks/#:~:text=Reef%20Sharks%20%7C%20WWF,prone%20to%20o

"

verfishing%20and%20targeting

Shark Species — Shark Research Institute. (n.d.). Shark Research Institute. https://www.sharks.org/species#:~:text=Every%20shark%20belongs%20to%20the,(8)%20orders%20of%20sharks

Anatomy of a shark tooth | The Dental Center of Indiana. (n.d.). The Dental Center of Indiana. https://www.dentalcenter-in.com/anatomy-shark-tooth

Sharks & Rays - Diet & Eating Habits | United Parks & Resorts. (n.d.). https://seaworld.org/animals/all-about/sharks-and-rays/diet/

Admin, A. W. (2021, December 7). Shark life Cycle & Shark reproduction: How do sharks reproduce? Active Wild. https://www.activewild.com/shark-life-cycle/

Welcome to Ocean of Know. (n.d.). https://oceanofk.org/tag/Tagmigrate/cfactorscause.html

The seven senses of sharks. (n.d.). https://shark.swiss/sharks/biology/7-senses

McCullough, D. (2020, July 27). 12 Sharks You should Know - Ocean Conservancy. Ocean Conservancy. https://oceanconservancy.org/blog/2019/07/29/12-sharks-to-know/?ea.tracking.id=23HPXGJAXX&utm_medium=PaidSearch&utm_source=GoogleGrants&utm_campaign=FY23&gad_source=1&gclid=Cj0KCQjwkdO0BhDxARIsANkNcrfBVTKXyMI524Dd3t3-HNTOwMGV1_sOWW2BzMZTIMmqmsSB5uFcWrwaAhJDEALw_wcB

Shark Academy: Everything about sharks! (n.d.). https://www.oceanic research.org/education/shark-academy/shark-academy.html

Sharks Hunting Techniques:Unveiling the Predator. (2024, April 23). Great White Shark Cage Diving Cape Town. https://apexpredators.co m/shark-hunting-techniques/#

MSN. (n.d.). https://www.msn.com/en-us/lifestyle/pets/these-are-th e-fastest-sharks-found-in-u-s-waters/ss-BB1pPEcQ#image=8

International Fund for Animal Welfare. (2023, August 28). The changing tides: Why are sharks increasingly approaching our shores? IFAW. https://www.ifaw.org/journal/why-sharks-increasingly-appro aching-shores

Which sharks are the most endangered? - Save Our Seas Foundation. (n.d.). Save Our Seas Foundation. https://saveourseas.com/worldofsh arks/which-sharks-are-the-most-endangered

Fisheries, N. (n.d.). Shark conservation. NOAA. https://www.fisheries. noaa.gov/international-affairs/shark-conservation